Keto Diet For Beginners:

21 Days For Rapid Weight Loss And Burn Fat Forever - Lose Up to 20 Pounds In 3 Weeks

By Melissa Hoffman

Table of Contents

INTRODUCTION

Do you ever get tired of working out only to realize that the days you spent sweating in the gym are not helping you to lose weight? Or maybe you have tried all the known fad diets out there, and none of them seem to work? Losing weight seems to get harder as we age but there is a way that allows anyone including you – yes, you! – to lose weight safely no matter how old you are.

If you have been watching the television or surfing the internet, you have probably encountered the term, ketogenic diet. Also known as the keto diet, the ketogenic diet is the hottest health trend today.

The ketogenic diet is easier to follow than other diet trends. It is a regimen that is very convenient and effective. It works with the principle of consuming foods that are high in healthy fats and protein so that the body enters the state of ketosis. Ketosis is when the body uses up stored fat as energy called ketones, in the absence of glucose (which we get from foods like sugars and carbs). When the body uses up stored fat, you end up losing weight in the process.

Let's simplify this. In a nutshell, the ketogenic diet is all about eating more fat to lose fat. Whoa! Is this for real? This is the truth. This diet encourages you to eat more fat so that you can lose fat. How is that even possible?

While it may sound like this is a new diet created in the 21st century, it really isn't. It has existed since the time of the cavemen. Yes! Since time immemorial, our ancestors have been consuming protein and fat sourced from animals that they have hunted, especially when times were tough, and they could not gather wild fruits and vegetables.

They didn't eat this way to lose weight, but as is a defense for survival. So, you see, our ancestors have been mostly eating under ketosis in order to survive.

While science has already explained how you can lose weight through the ketogenic diet, some people remain skeptical about it, especially when we have been taught in the past that eating high-fat foods like red meat, heavy cream, and butter are all fattening.

And although strange as it may seem, I still decided to follow the keto diet and I was astounded (and still am) by the results that I saw. Being a skeptic before, I used to weigh 205 pounds which made me obese considering that I have a small and short frame (I am only 5'5" tall, by the way). I was also borderline hypertensive and diabetic and these health conditions led me to think of drastic ways to lose weight fast. Until I found the ketogenic diet. I have lost 40 pounds within 8 months and I want you to experience the same results.

My goal here is to open your eyes and to let you understand the many benefits of the ketogenic diet. I know that you have some apprehensions about consuming fat to fight against fat but let me tell you that it works, and there is science behind it. Although I may not be a medical practitioner or a nutritionist, I am someone whose life became better because I followed the ketogenic diet.

I want you to enjoy its benefits as much as I have thus this book. I will give you the fundamentals of this diet so that you will understand how it works. I have simplified all information here so that ingesting it is easier. When I started with the ketogenic diet, I struggled personally because there was so many information – true and false – that are abundant on the internet. And so, to find the right balance, I have to experiment on myself. What I am giving you now is a simple step by step guide so that you can easily transition into this diet without having to find any difficulties.

After reading this book, you will better understand what the ketogenic diet is, how it works, which foods to eat and to which avoid. There are also tips to help you optimize your weight loss.

One thing I want you to remember, while the information found in this book can enrich your life, it is still up to you to stay motivated with this diet. After all, this diet is similar to a road less traveled. It can be hard but, in the end, it will be worth it.

So, if you think that there is no hope for you, then don't despair. If it worked for me, I am sure it will work for you. Read on and good luck!

To Start a New Lifestyle: What Is the Ketogenic Diet?

The ketogenic diet is also known as the low carb diet. It encourages the body to produce ketones from fats in the liver, which are then used by the body as a source of energy in the absence of glucose or sugar. When you eat foods that are high in carbohydrates, your body produces two biochemical compounds:

- Glucose: A simple sugar that is used by the cells as a source of energy.
- Insulin: A hormone that "pushes" the glucose from the bloodstream to the cells so that it [glucose] can be converted into energy.

Glucose is used as a primary source of energy, an excess of it is converted into fats and is stored in many organs such as the liver and adipose tissues. What if you could use up the stored fat as a source of energy and, in doing so, be able to deal with your weight issues? This is where the ketogenic diet comes in.

Ketosis is a natural process that the body goes through. It is part of our survival mechanisms allowing us to survive for days when our food intake is low. During this state, the body produces ketones from the breakdown of fats in the liver.

While it is convenient to fast so that the body can use up most of its fat reserves, not everyone can do fasting. By using and working on the principles of ketosis, the ketogenic diet mimics the metabolic state of ketosis without the hunger.

Look at it this way, if your diet is based primarily on carbs, this then drives the usual metabolic pathway, so you end up storing excess glucose into different parts of the body as fat. Carbs are neither good, nor bad but if you consume too many they can lead to problems like obesity, Type 2 diabetes, and cardiovascular disease.

By eating fewer carbs, you induce your body to the state of ketosis thus making it easier for the body to tap into the stored fat reserves it already has on hand. But getting yourself into the state of ketosis is never easy. Either you go on fasting for days or you cut down your carb intake to 50 grams daily, which is equivalent to around 5% of your total calories.

This can be achieved by changing your diet. Instead of taking in your usual diet, you can drive ketosis by eating more fat and protein. Your fat should be 60-75% of your daily calories while your protein intake should be 15-30% of your calories. This is equivalent to 1 large chicken breast and 5 small avocados each meal. Because fat is naturally filling, it will keep you full for a long time, so you will not feel the need to snack between meals.

The goal for the ketogenic diet is to get your body into the state of ketosis by breaking down fats into ketones as the primary source of fuel by eating the right amounts of food that support such metabolic pathway.

Is the Ketogenic Diet Really for You?

You have to remember that just like all other diet regimens, not everyone can follow a ketogenic diet. So, before you start this regimen, ask yourself if the ketogenic diet is really for you? Below are the things that you should consider to see if the ketogenic diet is for you.

- **How long can I follow this diet?** The ketogenic diet is not like your usual fad diet only lasting for a few weeks. In order to see results, it will take you months or even a year. So, if you are someone who cannot follow its principles long-term, then this diet is not for you.

- **Will the eating plan fit my food preference, budget needs, and culture?** If you follow a strict dietary guideline (veganism or vegetarianism) then you might need to tweak the ketogenic diet to fit your preferences. It may difficult, but not impossible. However, if you find it too much of a hassle to tweak the ketogenic meal plan to fit your preference, you might not enjoy this diet at all.

- **Do I have medical conditions that will put me at risk?** While the ketogenic diet has therapeutic effects to people who suffer from diabetes and cardiovascular diseases, it is not prescribed among people who suffer from kidney-related problems as the presence of protein and fats can be damaging to the kidneys.

The bottom line is that while the ketogenic diet is good for most people, it may not be advisable for some. So, before you ask yourself if this particular diet is for you, make sure that you seek advice from your nutritionist or physician.

How Exactly Does Ketogenic Work?

Since the carbohydrate intake for this particular diet is kept at a very low, carbs are practically absent thus the body is pushed to utilize other forms of energy in the form of fat.

In the absence of fat, the liver takes the fatty acids in the body then converts it into ketone bodies. You have to remember that the body just cannot take fat and use it in its raw form. It has to undergo different processes so that it can be utilized effectively by the body. This is the reason why it needs to convert it into ketone form. This process is called ketosis, and this is what the ketogenic diet is all about.

In a nutshell, there are three types of ketone bodies created during the break down of fatty acids and these include (1) acetoacetate, (2) beta-hydroxybutyric acid, and (3) acetone.

There are numerous benefits of the keto diet aside from weight loss and better energy levels.

- **Better blood sugar control:** The ketogenic diet lowers the blood sugar levels thus making it a great way to manage or even prevent diabetes. The thing is that the body takes a rest from producing insulin thus it can stabilize itself during ketosis.

- **Improved mental focus:** Several studies suggest that the ketogenic diet can increase health performance. Because this diet does not spike blood sugar levels, the brain is kept in a stable condition. Moreover, the brain simply loves ketones as its primary source of fuel.

- **Reduced cravings and hunger pains:** Fats are known to be filling, so this particular diet does not only curb your cravings but also reduces hunger pains.

- **Better cholesterol and blood pressure levels:** This particular diet regimen can improve triglyceride and cholesterol levels in the body. This reduces the risk of developing clogged arteries.

- **Clearer skin:** Didn't you know that the ketogenic diet can help improve the quality of your skin? Several studies suggest that people who follow the ketogenic diet often experience clearing of their acne and other skin anomalies. The ketogenic diet, aside from pushing ketosis, also drives the immune system into a frenzy thus it can help eliminate inflammation on the skin.

Before you can experience the many benefits of the ketogenic diet, it is important that you eat mostly fat. But how much fat is too much? When I first started, I had this misinformed idea that all I need to do is to eat all the fatty foods that I see. This was easy as pie, I said. And to tell you the truth, I see countless of dieters out there who make the same mistake that I did.

In order to succeed with the ketogenic diet, you don't need to eat a lot of fat. Rather, you need to smartly break down what you eat to 70-80% fat, 20-25% protein, and 5-10% carbohydrates.

You have to remember that the ratio varies depending on different people thus using an online calculator can greatly help! Make sure that you stick by your macros. The problem with most people is that they tend to eat more protein thinking that protein is always equivalent to fat. Well, not quite. Once you consume protein, the protein will be broken down into a process known as gluconeogenesis and it converts protein into carbs. So, you are back to square one.

To ensure that your body is constantly in the state of ketosis, you need to test the ketone levels in your body to know whether your body is still driving under this state or if you reverted back to your usual glucose-feeding metabolism.

There are several ways to test your body for the presence of ketones. Remember that when your body starts to burn off fats as its main energy source, ketones are spilled over into your blood and urine. And it is even present in you breathe! Since ketones are spilled all over the body, you can test either your urine or breath for its presence. You don't need to punch a tiny hole on your skin for blood testing.

Top 10 Foods You Definitely Must Avoid During Your Ketogenic Journey

The ketogenic diet is not rocket science. While it limits what type of foods that you can consume, it is not really difficult to eliminate certain food groups from your meals. Below are the types of foods that you need to avoid because they don't drive ketosis in the body.

- **Sugar of all types:** These include honey, maple syrup, white sugar, brown sugar, molasses, and fruit sugars.
- **Soda and fruit juice:** Soda and fruit juice (yes, even the natural kind) are full of sugar such as glucose and fructose so they can kick you out of ketosis.
- **Snacks:** Your favorite snacks such as donuts, cookies, cakes, and chocolate bars are strictly prohibited when you are following the ketogenic diet as they are loaded with a lot of sugar and trans-fat.
- **Grains:** Grains and starches are broken down into glucose thus they should be avoided at all cost. These include rice, oatmeal, rye, barley, wheat, corn, and basically all types of grains imaginable.
- **Fruits:** Fruits contain high amounts of fructose. Fruits that contain high amounts of sugar include watermelon, bananas, and many others.
- **Root vegetables:** Root vegetables like sweet potatoes, potatoes, parsnips, and carrots contain high amounts of starch, which can be converted into simple sugar.

- **Processed oils:** Ketogenic diet advocates the consumption of healthy fats, but it discourages the consumption of processed oils such as vegetable oil, canola oil, corn oil, and soy oil.
- **Alcoholic beverages:** Alcoholic beverages such as beer are high in sugar thus it is bad for ketosis.
- **Beans and legumes:** Beans and legumes are high in starch thus it is converted into glucose.

Top 10 Healthy Foods You Must Eat and Enjoy as A Successful Ketogenic Dieter

Staying in ketosis by eating the right foods is key to healthy weight loss. It is important that you consume more healthy fats than protein to stay in this particular metabolic pathway. I will constantly stress the importance of following the percentage of 5% carbs, 20% protein, and 75% fats. This means that you need to build your meals around low carb vegetables, healthy oils, and moderate protein. Below are the foods that you can consume to drive ketosis.

- **Good fats:** Remember that not all fats are created equally. While some fats are bad, some are very healthy for the body. You need to consume more good fats in the ketogenic diet. Your options include MCT oil, coconut oil, butter, olive oil, ghee, avocado oil, and other dairy sources like unprocessed cheese, and cream. Another good source of healthy fat is avocado.
- **Meat:** Choose from a selection of red meats, pork, chicken, turkey, and organ meats. Consume only a matchbox-sized portion for this diet regimen.

- **Fatty fish:** Fatty fish is a great source of fatty acids like Omega-3s that are precursors to ketones. Source them from trout, sardines, salmon, herring, and mostly cold-water fishes as they have more Omega-3s than other fishes.
- **Eggs:** Eggs are good sources of healthy fats and proteins.
- **Nuts and seeds:** Nuts and seeds are staple food items among keto dieters. Have a steady supply of brazil nuts, almond nuts, walnuts, pumpkin seeds, chia seeds, and cashew nuts.
- **Vegetables growing above ground:** Low carb vegetables in the form of leafy greens, cucumbers, onions, tomatoes, broccoli, cauliflower, and peppers are allowed in this diet. Basically, all vegetables growing above ground (except some squash varieties and tomatoes) are mostly made up of fiber, water, and less sugar.
- **Berries:** While most fruits are high discouraged while following the ketogenic diet, there are low sugar fruits that you are allowed to eat, and these include blueberries, limes, lemons, apples, and strawberries.
- **Sweeteners:** Sweeteners sourced from sugar with a high glycemic index is bad for the ketogenic diet. However, allowed sweeteners include stevia, monk fruits, and erythritol.
- **Water:** Water is the most acceptable beverage in the ketogenic diet because it contains no calories. But if you are not such a big fan of this particular diet, you can always opt for other beverages such as tea, coffee, and red wine (occasionally).
- **Bone broth:** Bone broth is not only hydrating but it is also chockfull of electrolytes, healthy fats, and nutrients. It is a great beverage to sip on the keto diet. For added fat, add a small dollop of butter to jump start ketosis.

8 Useful Tips to Help You Lose Up to 20 Pounds in 3 Week When You're on the Ketogenic Diet

Many people think that an all meat diet is very appealing but remember that the ketogenic diet does not work this way. It is important that you watch what you put into your plate so that your body can maintain ketosis. But while knowing how much fat, protein, and carbs is important, it is not enough to promote healthy weight loss. Thus, here are top tips on how to lose as much weight while following the ketogenic diet within the shortest possible time.

- **Weigh Your Food:** Being accurate about your macros is very crucial to the success of the ketogenic diet. Make sure that invest in a good food scale so that you can monitor your macro intake. So, avoid the guesswork and use a scale to measure your food. If you have more money to spare, buy scales that you can connect to apps and websites.

- **Drink Water:** Staying hydrated is one of the most important rules when it comes to following any kinds of diet regimen. Start your day by consuming at least 8 to 16 ounces of water to allow the body to begin its natural cycle. You need to drink half of your body weight in ounces. Thus, if you weigh 150 pounds, you need to drink 75 ounces of water for the entire day.

- **Exercise:** Remember that diet alone will not help you lose as much weight as you want. You can also do resistant training because it requires more protein to aid in muscle gain. This exercise is great for keeping your protein in check especially if you consumed more of it than fats. Make sure that you match this diet regimen with a high interval and high-intensity workout to improve your blood glucose levels. Exercise at least 25 minutes every day to see the best results.

- **Reduce Your Stress:** Stress can affect your hormone levels by causing your blood sugar level to rise thus increasing your cravings. Have you ever noticed why you often crave for sweets when you are stressed out? That's your hormone talking. While you cannot control the stress that comes your way, find ways on how to mitigate it. You can practice yoga, mindfulness, and breathing exercises to take away your stress.

- **Choose Quality Carbs:** Some of you may say that carb is carb no matter what form they exist in. But remember that not all carbs are created equally. There are carbs that are nutrient-rich and are found in non-starchy vegetables and some fruits. So, when making a meal plan, make sure that you use good quality carbs.

- **Stay Away from Diet Soda:** Just because it comes with the word "diet" with it does not mean that it is good for you. Diet soda uses a wide variety of sugar substitutes that tells your body that is has an overload of sugar thereby shutting the metabolism down. So, if you need to quench your thirst, drink sparkling water instead.

- **Get Enough Sleep:** Sleep is necessary in order for you to lose weight fast. Remember that the lack of sleep causes stress to the body. Stress, as I have discussed earlier can affect the hormone levels in your body thus increasing your cravings to constantly snack on food. So, make sure that you get at least 6 to 8 hours of sleep daily.

- **Intermittent Fasting:** If you truly want to lose weight fast with the ketogenic diet, you might want to consider pairing it with intermittent fasting. Intermittent fasting is when you fast for more than 12 hours so that your body will use up the stored fats as its primary fuel. Consume your keto-friendly meals within a short eating window time and the rest of the day should be dedicated to no food consumption so that your body can undergo the state of ketosis faster. For instance, you can go fasting from 2:00 pm to 8:00 am the following day. From 8:01 am to 1:59 pm, that is the only time you allow yourself to eat your meals.

10 Mistakes That Can Keep You from Being Successful on Your Ketogenic Diet

Numerous studies have pointed out the benefits of following the ketogenic diet. While some people experience successful results, others experience weight loss plateau. This term is defined as the certain stage wherein the body stops losing weight. Honestly, I have experienced weight loss plateau in the past and it is kind of frustrating that you worked so hard, but the extra pounds are not coming off.

If you have experienced or is experiencing this problem, have you ever wondered what is it that you are doing wrong? And you are actually right. There is something that you are doing wrong that is why this diet is not working for you now. Thus, below are common ketogenic diet mistakes that you need to be aware of and avoid.

- **Not Knowing Your Macros:** While calories count, your macros are more important when you follow the ketogenic diet. Remember that you need to make sure that you are eating the right amount of protein to prevent muscle loss but not too much to discourage ketosis. You can use a ketogenic diet calculator to figure out if you are following the recommended amounts of macros.

- **Avoiding Fiber:** Vegetables especially the non-starchy types will always have a place in this diet. Vegetables like bell peppers, zucchini, cauliflower, and broccoli are not only rich with micronutrients but they also contain a lot of fiber that will help regulate the absorption in your stomach.

- **Not Dealing with Stress:** Stress can affect your weight loss because it increases your cortisol levels. To cope up with the production of such hormone, the fat-burning mechanism of your body is affected, and it also increases your cravings for sugary foods. There are many ways for you to deal with stress and these include exercising, music therapy, or taking in supplements.

- **Eating Too Many Nuts:** While nuts are great snacks for keto dieters, too many of them will kick you out of ketosis. Nuts contain high amounts of calories. For instance, 100 grams of almonds is equivalent to 700 kcal and more than 70 grams of fat that is too much for people who want to lose weight. This does not mean that you have to avoid consumption of nuts. What you can do is to reduce your total intake to a few grams.

- **Eating Too Much Dairy:** Too much of a good thing can also be bad. Excessive consumption of dairy products can also kick off ketosis. Dairy products contain a type of protein that can lead to spikes in the insulin level. So, cut back on high-protein dairy such as cheese and yogurt. You can keep both cream and butter because they are low in that particular protein.

- **Eating Products that Are Labeled "Low Carb":** It is very easy to be deceived especially if the product comes with the label "low carb." The thing is that products that are labeled as such contain a lot of additives that are not good for the health.

- **Drinking Bulletproof Coffee:** Now this keto mistake caught me off guard. I have encountered bulletproof coffee when I did my initial research on the ketogenic diet. In fact, many health gurus swear by it. While it can drive ketosis, I believe that bulletproof coffee has very low nutrients. I mean, I prefer getting my calories from real and nutritious keto-friendly foods.

- **Not Planning Your Meals:** When you fail to plan, then you plan to fail. Not planning your diet can easily kick you out of ketosis. Planning your meals in advance is really helpful so that you avoid excessive snacking or getting involved in binging accidents. While it is impractical to keep track of your diet forever, you can do meal prepping so that it omits the need for you to eat anything randomly.

- **Not Getting Enough Exercise:** Not getting enough exercise is counterproductive for the keto diet. Choose the right type of exercise depending on your goals. For you to reap the most health benefits of exercise, you can do light cardio exercises as it is good for both the mind and heart. Doing weight training and high-intensity workout can also build your muscles. On the other hand, post-workout nutrition is also very important to help you succeed with the ketogenic diet. Make sure that you avoid eating foods that are high in fat exercising.

- **Having Cheat Meals:** A part of you might be telling yourself to go and grab a burger after a week of dieting because you deserve a reward. But let me tell you that having a cheat day can kick your body out of ketosis, which is something that you worked hard for in such a long time. It is a counterproductive move for your diet.

Keto Meal Prep Breakfast Recipes

Buttered Basil on Scrambled Egg

Servings per Recipe: 2
Cooking Time: 8 minutes

Ingredients:

- 2 oz. butter
- 4 eggs
- 4 tbsp coconut cream or coconut milk or sour cream
- 4 tbsp fresh basil
- salt

Directions:

1. Place a nonstick pan on low heat and melt butter.
2. Meanwhile, in a small bowl whisk eggs, coconut cream, basil and salt. Pour in pan.
3. With a spatula, stir eggs until scrambled and cooked to desired doneness.
4. Let it cool. Evenly divide into suggested servings and place in meal prep containers.

Nutrition Information:

Calories per serving: 427; Protein: 13g; Fat: 42g; Carbohydrates: 3g; Fiber: 1g

Mushroom Omelet Keto Approved

Servings per Recipe: 3

Cooking Time: 12 minutes

Ingredients:

- 9 eggs
- 2/3 yellow onion
- 3 oz. butter, for frying
- 3 oz. shredded cheese
- 9 mushrooms
- salt and pepper

Directions:

1. Place a nonstick skillet on medium heat.
2. Meanwhile, in a large bowl whisk well eggs, salt, and pepper.
3. Add butter to pan and let it melt.
4. Add mushrooms and onion. Sauté for 3 minutes. Pour in eggs.
5. Cover and lower heat to medium low. Cook for 8 minutes.
6. Add cheese on top. Cover and continue to cook for another 3 minutes.
7. Fold in half and continue cooking until eggs are golden brown underneath.
8. Let it cool. Evenly divide into suggested servings and place in meal prep containers.

Nutrition Information:

Calories per serving: 510; Protein: 25g; Fat: 43g; Carbohydrates: 5g; Fiber: 1g

Caprese Omelet Keto Approved

Servings per Recipe: 3
Cooking Time: 15 minutes

Ingredients:

- 9 eggs
- 1½ tbsp fresh basil or dried basil
- 3 tbsp olive oil
- 4½ oz. cherry tomatoes cut in halves or tomatoes cut in halves
- 7½ oz. fresh mozzarella cheese
- salt and pepper

Directions:

1. Place a large nonstick pan on medium heat and heat oil.
2. Meanwhile, in a large bowl whisk eggs. Season with salt and pepper. Mix well.
3. Add sliced tomatoes in pan and sauté for 4 minutes.
4. Pour eggs in pan. Lower heat to medium low, cover and cook for 5 minutes.
5. Add cheese and continue cooking while covered until omelet is set, around 8 minutes more.
6. Let it cool. Evenly divide into suggested servings and place in meal prep containers.

Nutrition Information:

Calories per serving: 534; Protein: 33g; Fat: 43g; Carbohydrates: 5g; Fiber: 1g

Keto Approved Pancakes

Servings per Recipe: 3

Cooking Time: 10 minutes

Ingredients:

- 8 eggs
- 2¾ oz. pork rinds
- 4 tsp ground cinnamon
- 4 tsp maple extract
- 8 tbsp coconut oil, for frying
- 8 tbsp unsweetened cashew milk
- 2 tbsp coconut oil

Directions:

1. In a blender, pulse pork rids until it becomes a fine powder. Add remaining ingredients and blend well to combine.
2. Place a small nonstick skillet on medium heat and heat a tablespoon of coconut oil.
3. Once hot add ¼ cup of batter and cook for two minutes. Flip pancake and cook the other side for another minute.
4. Repeat process until you have used up all the batter.
5. Let it cool. Evenly divide into suggested servings and place in meal prep containers.

Nutrition Information:

Calories per serving: 510; Protein: 24g; Fat: 43g; Carbohydrates: 4g; Fiber: 2g

Keto Approved Easy Egg Muffins

Servings per Recipe: 6

Cooking Time: 18 minutes

Ingredients:

- 12 eggs
- 2 scallions, finely chopped
- 2 tbsp red pesto or green pesto (optional)
- 5 oz. air-dried chorizo or cooked bacon, chopped or crumbled
- 6 oz. shredded cheese
- salt and pepper

Directions:

1. Lightly grease 12 muffin tins and preheat oven to 350°F.
2. Evenly sprinkle scallions and chorizo or bacon on bottom of tins.
3. In a bowl, whisk eggs. Season with pepper and salt. Add pesto and cheese. Mix well.
4. Evenly pour eggs in muffin tins.
5. Pop in the oven and bake for 18 minutes or until set.
6. Let it cool. Evenly divide into suggested servings and place in meal prep containers.

Nutrition Information:

Calories per serving: 336; Protein: 23g; Fat: 26g; Carbohydrates: 2g; Fiber: 0g

KETO ASPARAGUS FRITTATA

Servings per Recipe: 4
Cooking Time: 22 minutes

Ingredients:

- 8 Eggs
- 1 Tablespoon Olive Oil
- 2 Teaspoons Butter
- 1/2-Pound Asparagus, Trimmed, Cut Into 1-Inch Pieces
- 1/2 Cup Grated Parmesan Cheese, or More to Taste
- 7 Tablespoons Milk
- Salt and Freshly Ground Black Pepper to Taste

Directions:

1. Place a nonstick pan on medium heat and add oil.
2. Once oil is hot, sauté asparagus for 10 minutes or until tender.
3. Meanwhile, in a bowl whisk eggs until frothy. Season with pepper and salt. Stir in milk and cheese.
4. Pour egg mixture into pan with asparagus, lower heat to medium low, cover pan, and cook for 12 minutes or until eggs are set.
5. Let it cool. Evenly divide into suggested servings and place in meal prep containers.

Nutrition Information:

Calories per serving: 242; Protein: 17.1g; Fat: 17.6g; Carbohydrates: 4.6g; Fiber: 1.2g

Keto-Approved Blueberry Pancakes

Servings per Recipe: 2

Cooking Time: 5 minutes

Ingredients:

- 1 egg
- 1 pinch salt
- 1 tbsp almond milk
- 1 tbsp coconut oil
- 1 tsp coconut flour
- 1/16 tsp Stevia
- 1/4 cup almond flour
- 1/4 tsp baking powder
- 1/4 tsp cinnamon
- ¼ cup blueberries

Directions:

1. In blender, mix all ingredients except for blueberries and coconut oil. Blend until smooth and creamy.
2. In a small nonstick pan on medium heat, heat ½ of the oil.
3. Once oil is hot, add half of the batter. Drop half of the blueberries in a single layer in the cooking pancake. Cook for 1 ½ minutes. Flip pancake and cook for another minute.
4. Repeat process to remaining batter.
5. Let it cool. Evenly divide into suggested servings and place in meal prep containers.

Nutrition Information:

Calories per serving: 415; Protein: 15g; Fat: 35g; Carbohydrates: 10.5g; Fiber: 3.5g

Slow Cooked Egg Casserole

Servings per Recipe: 6
Cooking Time: 5 hours

Ingredients:

- 12 eggs, whisked
- ½ cup feta cheese
- ½ cup milk
- ½ cup sun dried tomatoes
- ½ teaspoon salt
- 1 cup baby Bella mushrooms (sliced)
- 1 tablespoon red onion, chopped
- 1 teaspoon black pepper
- 1 teaspoon garlic, minced
- 2 cups spinach

Directions:

1. In a large bowl, whisk eggs.
2. Season with pepper and salt.
3. Mix in milk, garlic, and red onion.
4. Mix thoroughly in spinach, mushrooms, and sun-dried tomatoes.
5. With cooking spray, grease sides and bottom of a slow cooker.
6. Cover and cook on low for 5 hours or until eggs are set.
7. Let it cool. Evenly divide into suggested servings and place in meal prep containers.

Nutrition Information:

Calories per serving: 191; Protein: 15.0g; Fat: 12.0g; Carbohydrates: 6.1g; Fiber: 1.1g

Breakfast Cauliflower Hash

Servings per Recipe: 2
Cooking Time: 15 minutes

Ingredients:

- 8-ounce shaved red pastrami, chopped into 1-inch slices
- ½ green bell pepper, chopped into ¼-inch pieces
- 1 teaspoon Cajun seasoning
- 1-pound bag frozen cauliflower, chopped roughly
- 2 tablespoons minced garlic
- ½ onion, chopped into ¼-inch pieces
- 2 tablespoons olive oil

Directions:

1. In a blender or food processor, add roughly chopped cauliflower and burr until you have even rice-like flakes. Set aside.
2. Place a medium nonstick pan on medium heat and add oil.
3. Once oil is hot, stir in garlic and cook until lightly browned, around 2 minutes.
4. Stir in onions and Cajun seasoning. Sauté for a minute.
5. Add burred cauliflower and sauté for 5 minutes or until lightly browned.
6. Stir in green pepper and pastrami.
7. Continue sautéing for another 5 minutes and then turn off heat.
8. Let it cool. Evenly divide into suggested servings and place in meal prep containers.

Nutrition Information:

Calories per serving: 231; Protein:6.7 g; Fat: 14.6g; Carbohydrates: 23.5g; Fiber: 7.3g

Keto Approved Coco-Porridge

Servings per Recipe: 2

Cooking Time: 10 minutes

Ingredients:

- 2 eggs
- 1 tsp ground psyllium husk
- 2 tablespoons coconut flour
- 2-ounces butter
- 8 tablespoons coconut cream
- Salt to taste

Directions:

1. Place a medium pot on medium heat.
2. Melt butter. Once melted add all ingredients and mix well.
3. Bring to a simmer while stirring pot every now and then.
4. Once simmering, continuously mix pot until desired thickness is achieved.
5. Turn off heat.
6. Let it cool. Evenly divide into suggested servings and place in meal prep containers.

Nutrition Information:

Calories per serving: 364; Protein: 8.1g; Fat: 30.4g; Carbohydrates: 15.5g; Fiber: 0.7g

Mexican Egg Casserole

Servings per Recipe: 8

Cooking Time: 20 minutes

Ingredients:

- 10 eggs
- ¼ teaspoon pepper
- ¼ teaspoon salt
- ½ teaspoon coriander
- ½ teaspoon garlic powder
- 1 cup milk
- 1 cup pepper jack
- 1 cup salsa
- 1 teaspoon chili powder
- 1 teaspoon cumin
- 12-ounces Jones Dairy Farm Pork Sausage Roll

Directions:

1. Place a heavy-bottomed pot on medium heat.
2. Once pot is hot, add pork sausage and cook until no longer pink.
3. Stir in chili powder, cumin, coriander, and garlic powder and sauté for a minute.
4. Pour in salsa, mix well, and press warming button.
5. Meanwhile, in a large bowl whisk well eggs, milk, pepper, and salt.
6. Pour egg mixture into Instant Pot and mix well.
7. Add cheese, whisk well.
8. Cover and cook for 8 minutes on medium heat.
9. Lower heat to medium low and continue cooking until casserole has set, around 12 to 15 minutes. Do not open lid.
10. Let it cool. Evenly divide into suggested servings and place in meal prep containers.

Nutrition Information:

Calories per serving: 400; Protein: 22.4g; Fat: 30.1g; Carbohydrates: 6.5g; Fiber: 1g

Mushroom-Kale Frittata

Servings per Recipe: 2

Cooking Time: 17 minutes

Ingredients:

- 4 large eggs, beaten
- 2 tablespoons ghee
- 2 teaspoons minced garlic
- 1 cup mushrooms, sliced
- 1 cup chopped kale
- Pepper and salt to taste

Directions:

1. Place a medium skillet on medium heat and heat oil.
2. Meanwhile, in a bowl whisk well the eggs. Season with pepper and salt to taste.
3. Sauté garlic for a minute.
4. Add mushrooms and sauté for 5 minutes.
5. Add kale and sauté for 2 minutes or until nearly wilted.
6. Pour in eggs, cover, and cook for 5 minutes.
7. Lower heat to medium low and cook for another 5 minutes or until set.
8. Let it cool. Evenly divide into suggested servings and place in meal prep containers.

Nutrition Information:

Calories per serving: 238; Protein: 4g; Fat: 22.6g; Carbohydrates: 2.8g; Fiber: 1.4g

Keto Spinach Frittata

Servings per Recipe: 4
Cooking Time: 21 minutes

Ingredients:

- 8 large eggs, beaten
- ¼ onion, diced
- 1 cup almond milk, unsweetened
- 2 cups spinach
- 4 large egg whites, beaten
- 1 tbsp oil

Directions:

1. Place a medium cast-iron pan on medium high heat and heat oil.
2. In a mixing bowl, combine the eggs, egg whites, and almond milk. Season with salt and pepper to taste.
3. Add onions to pan and sauté for 3 minutes.
4. Stir in spinach and sauté for a minute. Then, evenly spread all over the pan.
5. Pour in egg mixture.
6. Cover and cook for 8 minutes.
7. Lower heat to medium low and continue cooking for another 10 minutes or until Frittata is set.
8. Let it cool. Evenly divide into suggested servings and place in meal prep containers.

Nutrition Information:

Calories per serving: 234; Protein: 18.6g; Fat: 15.0g; Carbohydrates: 5.1g; Fiber: 0.4g

Breakfast Taco on a Skillet

Servings per Recipe: 6

Cooking Time: 50 minutes

Ingredients:

- 10 large eggs
- 1 1/2 cups shredded sharp cheddar cheese, divided
- 1 roma tomato, diced
- 1/4 cup heavy cream
- 1/4 cup salsa
- 1/4 cup sliced black olives
- 1/4 cup sour cream
- 1-pound ground beef
- 2 green onions, sliced
- 2 tablespoons torn fresh cilantro (optional)
- 2/3 cup water
- 4 tablespoons Taco Seasoning

Directions:

1. Place a large cast-iron pan on medium-high heat.
2. Once hot, add beef and sauté until browned, around 10 minutes. Drain excess oil.
3. Add water and taco seasoning to pan and mix well. Lower heat to medium and continue cooking until water has evaporated, around 10 minutes more.
4. Preheat oven to 375°F.
5. Meanwhile, in a bowl whisk the eggs. Stir in heavy cream and a cup of cheese. Mix well.
6. Transfer half of the meat on a plate.
7. Pour egg in pan and mix well.
8. Pop the pan in the oven and bake until cooked through, around 30 minutes.

9. Remove from oven and top with salsa, sour cream, green onion, cilantro, olives, tomato, and the remaining cheese.
10. Let it cool. Evenly divide into suggested servings and place in meal prep containers.

Nutrition Information:

Calories per serving: 459; Protein: 38.5g; Fat: 29.4g; Carbohydrates: 7.2g; Fiber: 1.5g

Keto Approved Homemade Hot Pockets

Servings per Recipe: 4
Cooking Time: 30 minutes

Ingredients:

- 4 eggs large
- 4 tablespoon unsalted butter
- 6 slices bacon cooked
- 1 1/2 cup Mozzarella
- 2/3 cup almond flour

Directions:

1. Place a nonstick skillet and place on medium heat. Cook bacon for 5 minutes, divide into 4 equal parts and set aside.
2. Whisk eggs in a bowl, season with salt and pepper. Cook in same pan. Transfer to a plate and divide evenly into four.
3. Preheat oven to 400°F.
4. In a microwave safe bowl, melt mozzarella and butter. Stir in flour and mix well.
5. Roll dough in two sheets of wax paper into ¼-inch thickness. Divide into 4 equal sizes.
6. Place ¼ egg and ¼ bacon in middle of one dough. Fold in half and seal edges. Poke the middle in several spots to vent hot pockets. Repeat process for remaining dough.
7. Place on a lightly greased baking sheet and bake in the oven until golden brown, around 20 minutes.
8. Let it cool. Evenly divide into suggested servings and place in meal prep containers.

Nutrition Information:

Calories per serving: 455; Protein: 25.0g; Fat: 38.0g; Carbohydrates: 3.5g; Fiber: 0.5g

Keto-Approved Burrito Breakfast Bowl

Servings per Recipe: 2

Cooking Time: 20 minutes

Ingredients:

- 3 eggs beaten
- 1 tbsp keto taco seasoning
- 1 tsp ghee
- 1/2-pound lean ground beef
- 1/3 head cauliflower riced
- 2 tbsp cilantro chopped
- 3/4 cup water
- sea salt & pepper to taste

Directions:

1. Place a large nonstick skillet on medium high heat.
2. Sauté ground beef for 3 minutes. Season with taco seasoning and continue cooking until liquid has evaporated, around 8 minutes. Discard any fat dripping. Transfer to a large bowl.
3. In same pan, sauté cauliflower. Season with salt and cilantro. Continue sautéing for 4 minutes or until tender. Transfer to same bowl with ground beef.
4. In same pan, melt ghee. Pour in eggs and scramble for 3 minutes.
5. Return ground beef and cauliflower in pan and continue stirring and cooking for a minute or two.
6. Let it cool. Evenly divide into suggested servings and place in meal prep containers.

Nutrition Information:

Calories per serving: 299; Protein: 34.0g; Fat: 14.0g; Carbohydrates: 5.0g; Fiber: 1.0g

Egg Cups Wrapped in Zucchini

Servings per Recipe: 6

Cooking Time: 40 minutes

Ingredients:

- 8 eggs
- 1 cup Pinch red pepper flakes
- 1 cup shredded cheddar
- 1/2 cup cherry tomatoes, quartered
- 1/2 cup heavy cream
- 1/2 tsp dried oregano
- ¼-lb ham, chopped
- 2 zucchini, peeled into strips
- Cooking spray, for pan
- Freshly ground black pepper
- Kosher salt

Directions:

1. With cooking spray, lightly grease 12 muffin tins. Preheat oven to 400°F.
2. To form cups, line the muffin tins with the zucchini strips. Ensuring that it forms like a muffin cup.
3. Sprinkle cherry tomatoes and ham in the cups.
4. Whisk well heavy cream, eggs, red pepper flakes, and oregano in a medium bowl. Season with pepper and salt. Mix well.
5. Evenly divide egg mixture into the 12 muffin tins.
6. Pop in the oven and bake for 30 minutes or until eggs are set.
7. Let it cool. Evenly divide into suggested servings and place in meal prep containers.

Nutrition Information:

Calories per serving: 337; Protein: 21.8g; Fat: 24.9g; Carbohydrates: 6.7g; Fiber: 1.0g

Traditional Scotch Eggs Recipe

Servings per Recipe: 5
Cooking Time: 15 minutes

Ingredients:

- ½ teaspoon paprika powder
- 1 ½ pounds ground pork
- 1 egg, beaten
- 1 garlic clove minced
- 5 eggs, hardboiled and peeled

Directions:

1. Place a steam rack in the Instant Pot and pour a cup of water.
2. Combine the beaten egg, ground pork, garlic, and paprika in a mixing bowl. Season with salt and pepper to taste.
3. Divide the meat mixture into 5 balls.
4. Flatten the balls with your hands and place an egg at the center. Cover the egg with the meat mixture. Do the same thing with the other balls.
5. Allow to set in the fridge for at least 2 hours.
6. Place the frozen meat on the steam rack.
7. Close the lid and make sure that the vent points to "Sealing."
8. Press the "Steam" button and adjust the time to 15 minutes.
9. Do natural pressure release and allow the balls to cool in the fridge for an hour.
10. Take the steam rack out and thrown away the water.
11. Without the lid on, press the Sauté button and allow the balls to sear on all sides until lightly golden.
12. Let it cool. Evenly divide into suggested servings and place in meal prep containers.

Nutrition Information:

Calories per serving: 561; Protein: 30.4g; Fat: 47.1g; Carbohydrates: 1.6g; Fiber: 0.5g

Keto Meal Prep Lunch Recipes

Hashed Brussels Sprouts

Servings per Recipe: 4

Cooking Time: 40 minutes

Ingredients:

- 4 large eggs
- 6 slices bacon, cut into 1" pieces
- 1-lb Brussels sprouts, trimmed and quartered
- kosher salt
- Freshly ground black pepper
- 2 tbsp water
- 2 garlic cloves, minced
- 1/2 onion, chopped
- 1/4 tsp red pepper flakes

Directions:

1. On medium heat, place a nonstick pan and crisp fry bacon. Once done, transfer to a plate and pat away the oil with a paper towel.
2. In same pan with bacon grease, sauté onion for a minute.
3. Stir in Brussels sprouts and cook for 3 minutes.
4. Season with red pepper flakes, pepper, and salt.
5. Add water and continue cooking until liquid has evaporated.
6. Create four holes in the pan and crack eggs. Season eggs with pepper and salt.
7. Cover and continue cooking until eggs are cooked to desired doneness.
8. Let it cool. Evenly divide into suggested servings and place in meal prep containers.

Nutrition Information:

Calories per serving: 270; Protein: 11.7g; Fat: 20.2g; Carbohydrates: 12.9g; Fiber: 4.6g

Stir-Fried Ground Beef

Servings per Recipe: 2

Cooking Time: 15 minutes

Ingredients:

- 1-lb ground beef
- ½ cup broccoli, chopped
- ½ of medium-sized onions, chopped
- ½ of medium-sized red bell pepper, chopped
- 1 tbsp cayenne pepper (optional)
- 1 tbsp Chinese five spices
- 1 tbsp coconut oil
- 2 kale leaves, chopped
- 5 medium-sized mushrooms, sliced

Directions:

1. In a skillet, heat the coconut oil over medium high heat.
2. Sauté the onions for one minute and add the vegetables while stirring constantly.
3. Add the ground beef and the spices.
4. Cook for two minutes and reduce the heat to medium.
5. Cover the skillet and continue to cook the beef and vegetables for another 10 minutes.
6. Let it cool. Evenly divide into suggested servings and place in meal prep containers.

Nutrition Information:

Calories per serving: 592; Protein: 63.6g; Fat: 33.0g; Carbohydrates: 9.3g; Fiber: 3.1g

Asian Beef Short Ribs

Servings per Recipe: 4

Cooking Time: 12 Hours

Ingredients:

- 2 pounds beef short ribs
- 1 cup water
- 1 onion, diced
- 1 tablespoon Szechuan peppercorns
- 2 tablespoons curry powder
- 3 tablespoons coconut aminos
- 6-pieces star anise
- 6 tablespoons sesame oil
- Salt and pepper to taste

Directions:

1. Place all ingredients except for the sesame oil in the Instant Pot.
2. Close the lid and make sure that the steam release valve is set to "Venting."
3. Press the "Slow Cook" button and adjust the cooking time to 12 hours.
4. Once cooked, drizzled with sesame oil.
5. Let it cool. Evenly divide into suggested servings and place in meal prep containers.

Nutrition Information:

Calories per serving: 592; Protein: 46.7g; Fat: 43.6g; Carbohydrates: 5.8g; Fiber: 3.2g

TRADITIONAL FRIED CHICKEN

Servings per Recipe: 8

Cooking Time: 40 minutes

Ingredients:

- 2 large eggs
- 8 chicken pieces, skin on and bone in
- ¼ cup heavy cream
- ¼ cup water
- ½ cup parmesan cheese
- ½ tsp onion powder
- ¾ cup plain whey protein
- 1 cup crushed pork rinds
- 1 tbsp oat fiber
- 1 tsp seasoning
- 1/8 tsp coarse black pepper

Directions:

1. Mix all the dry ingredients in a Ziploc bag. Set aside.
2. In a separate bowl, mix together water, eggs and cream.
3. Toss the chicken pieces in the egg mixture.
4. Pick the meat and drop to the bowl of dry ingredients. Toss the bag to evenly coat the chicken. Set aside.
5. Heat a fryer that has ¾-inchese of oil in high heat.
6. Place the chicken in the hot oil and cook for 30 to 40 minutes until golden brown.
7. Let it cool. Evenly divide into suggested servings and place in meal prep containers.

Nutrition Information:

Calories per serving: 560; Protein: 63.9g; Fat: 29.6g; Carbohydrates: 6.2g; Fiber: 0.2g

Asian-Inspired Keto Pork chops

Servings per Recipe: 4
Cooking Time: 15 minutes

Ingredients:

- 4 boneless pork chops
- ½ tbsp Sambal chili paste
- ½ tbsp sugar-free ketchup
- ½ tsp five spice powder
- ½ tsp pepper corn
- 1 ½ tsp soy sauce
- 1 medium star anise
- 1 stalk lemongrass, peeled and diced
- 1 tbsp almond flour
- 1 tbsp fish sauce
- 1 tsp Sesame oil
- 4 halved garlic cloves, crushed

Directions:

1. Place the pork chops on a stable working surface. With a rolling pin wrapped in wax paper, pound the pork chop to ½ inch thickness.
2. Ground the star anise and pepper corns using a mortar and pestle. Add the lemon grass and garlic and continue pounding until they form a puree.
3. Add soy sauce, fish sauce, five spice powder and sesame oil. Mix well. This will be the marinade.
4. Put the pork chops on a baking tray and add marinade. Toss or massage the marinade to the pork chops. Let it sit for 2 hours at room temperature.
5. Using a skillet, heat the pan and put a little amount oil for frying.
6. Separately, coat the pork chops with almond flour. Put the pork chops to the pan and sear both sides.

7. Cook for two minutes for each side until it becomes golden brown in color.
8. Meanwhile, make the sauce by mixing the sugar-free ketchup and sambal chili paste.
9. Let it cool. Evenly divide into suggested servings, and place in meal prep containers with sauce on the side.

Nutrition Information:

Calories per serving: 272; Protein: 43.2g; Fat: 8.3g; Carbohydrates: 4.2g; Fiber: 0.6g

Steamed Mahi-Mahi with Hummus

Servings per Recipe: 2

Cooking Time: 30 minutes

Ingredients:

- 2 filets Mahi Mahi fish
- Fresh coriander
- 2 tbsp lime, squeezed
- 2 tsp Philadelphia cheese
- 4 tbsp hummus
- Salt and pepper to taste

Directions:

1. Place Mahi mahi on a heat proof dish that fits in your steamer.
2. Season with pepper, salt, and lime.
3. Sprinkle cilantro on top. Securely cover top of dish with foil and place in steamer.
4. Steam for 30 minutes.
5. Let it cool. Evenly divide into suggested servings and place in meal prep containers.

Nutrition Information:

Calories per serving: 273; Protein: 24.0g; Fat: 14.4g; Carbohydrates: 12.0g; Fiber: 1.9g

Baked Herby Salmon

Servings per Recipe: 4
Cooking Time: 15 minutes

Ingredients:

- 2 pounds salmon fillet
- ¼ tsp tarragon
- ¼ tsp thyme
- ½ cup coconut aminos
- ½ tsp basil
- ½ tsp ground ginger
- ½ tsp rosemary
- 1 tsp minced garlic
- 1 tsp dried oregano
- 4 tsp sesame oil

Directions:

1. In a Ziploc back, place the sesame oil, soy sauce and spices and shake thoroughly until well combined. Put the salmon pieces in the Ziploc bag. Refrigerate the salmon with the marinade for 4 hours.
2. Preheat the oven to 350°F. Place the marinated salmon on a baking pan lined with aluminum foil.
3. Bake the marinated salmon for 15 minutes.
4. Let it cool. Evenly divide into suggested servings and place in meal prep containers.

Nutrition Information:

Calories per serving: 396; Protein: 47.1g; Fat: 20.9g; Carbohydrates: 1.8g; Fiber: 0.5g

Chicken Coconut Curry

Servings per Recipe: 4

Cooking Time: 25 minutes

Ingredients:

- 1 ½ tsps curry powder
- ½ onion, sliced
- 1-lb chicken breast, cut into bite-sized pieces
- 1 tbsp avocado oil
- 2 tsps garlic, minced
- 1 tbsp coconut aminos
- 1 tbsp ginger, minced
- 1 ½ cups coconut milk
- 1/8 tsp salt

Directions:

1. On medium high heat, place a large nonstick saucepan and heat avocado oil.
2. Add chicken and stir fry for 9 minutes or until chicken is no longer pink. Transfer chicken to a plate leaving oil in pan.
3. Stir fry garlic, ginger, and onion for 3 minutes.
4. Season with curry, coconut aminos, and salt. Sauté for a minute.
5. Return chicken and sauté for 3 minutes.
6. Pour coconut milk, bring to a boil then low heat to a simmer. Simmer for 10 minutes.
7. Let it cool. Evenly divide into suggested servings and place in meal prep containers.

Nutrition Information:

Calories per serving: 328; Protein: 27.1g; Fat: 23.6g; Carbohydrates: 3.8g; Fiber: 0.5g

Greek Styled Lamb Chops

Servings per Recipe: 4
Cooking Time: 6 minutes

Ingredients:

- 1 tbsp black pepper
- 1 tbsp dried oregano
- 1 tbsp minced garlic
- 2 tbsps lemon juice
- 2 tsp oil
- 2 tsp salt
- 8 pcs of lamb loin chops, around 4 oz

Directions:

1. In a big bowl or dish, combine the black pepper, salt, minced garlic, lemon juice and oregano. Then rub it equally on all sides of the lamb chops.
2. Then place a skillet on high heat. After a minute, coat skillet with the cooking spray and place the lamb chops. Sear lamb chops for a minute on each side.
3. Lower heat to medium, continue cooking lamb chops for 2-3 minutes per side or until desired doneness is reached.
4. Let it cool. Evenly divide into suggested servings and place in meal prep containers.

Nutrition Information:

Calories per serving: 457; Protein: 63.0g; Fat: 9.0g; Carbohydrates: 4.0g; Fiber: 1.0g

Chicken Puttanesca

Servings per Recipe: 4

Cooking Time: 35 minutes

Ingredients:

- ¼ cup extra virgin olive oil
- ½ cup assorted Italian olives, pitted and coarsely chopped
- ½ tsp crushed red chili flakes
- 1 lb fresh tomatoes, diced
- 1 small red onion, diced
- 4 boneless chicken breasts
- 4 pieces boneless anchovy filets, coarsely chopped
- 4 pieces garlic cloves, minced
- Pepper and salt to taste

Directions:

1. On high heat, place an oven proof, large skillet.
2. Prepare chicken breasts by seasoning with pepper and salt and greasing with 2 tbsps extra virgin olive oil.
3. Sear chicken on hot skillet around 2 minutes per side or until golden brown on each side. When done searing, lower heat to medium-low, cover and cook until juices run clear. Around 6-8 minutes.
4. Remove from pan and transfer chicken to a platter.
5. On same skillet on medium heat, sauté chili flakes, capers, olives, anchovies, onions, garlic and remaining oil for 2 to 3 minutes.
6. Add tomatoes and season with pepper and salt. Increase heat to high and cook until you have a thick sauce, around 10 to 12 minutes.
7. Pour sauce on top of chicken.
8. Let it cool. Evenly divide into suggested servings and place in meal prep containers.

Nutrition Information:

Calories per serving: 349; Protein: 33.0g; Fat: 21.0g; Carbohydrates: 7.0g; Fiber: 2.0g

Sun Dried Tomato and Artichoke Chicken

Servings per Recipe: 4
Cooking Time: 25 minutes

Ingredients:

- ¼ cup sun dried tomato pesto
- 1 14.5-oz can diced tomatoes with green peppers and onions
- 1 14-oz can artichoke hearts in water, drained and quartered
- 2 tsps olive oil
- 4 skinless, boneless chicken breast halves
- Pepper and salt to taste

Directions:

1. With pepper and salt, season all sides of chicken.
2. On medium high heat, place a large saucepan and heat oil until hot.
3. Add chicken and brown each side, around 5 minutes per side. Once done, transfer chicken to a plate.
4. In same pan, add tomatoes and stir fry for a minute. Scrape all sides of pan to incorporate browned bits.
5. Add artichokes and pesto. Cook and stir for a minute.
6. Return chicken to pan, cover and simmer for 10 minutes on medium heat.
7. Let it cool. Evenly divide into suggested servings and place in meal prep containers.

Nutrition Information:

Calories per serving: 322; Protein: 34.0g; Fat: 15.0g; Carbohydrates: 20.0g; Fiber: 6.0g

Zucchini Noodles with Sausages

Servings per Recipe: 2

Cooking Time: 10 minutes

Ingredients:

- 2 cups of chicken sausages, sliced
- 2 large zucchinis
- 2 tablespoons coconut oil
- 4 garlic cloves, minced
- Salt and pepper to taste

Directions:

1. Make the zucchini noodles. You can do this with a mandolin, but you can also slice the zucchini into thin long strips using a knife.
2. In a skillet, heat up the oil over medium heat and sauté the garlic for three minutes while stirring constantly. Add the sausages and cook for another five minutes or until the sausages are cooked through.
3. Add the zucchini and season with salt and pepper to taste.
4. Let it cool. Evenly divide into suggested servings and place in meal prep containers.

Nutrition Information:

Calories per serving: 178; Protein: 4.3g; Fat: 14.2g; Carbohydrates: 12.9g; Fiber: 3.7g

Keto-Approved Beef Ragu

Servings per Recipe: 2

Cooking Time: 10 minutes

Ingredients:

- 1/4-pound ground beef
- 1 teaspoon salt
- 2 large zucchinis, cut into noodle strips
- 1 tablespoon ghee or butter
- 4 tablespoons fresh parsley, chopped

Directions:

1. Heat the ghee in a skillet under medium flame and cook the ground beef until thoroughly cooked, around 5 minutes.
2. Add the packaged pesto sauce and season with salt. Add the chopped parsley and cook for three more minutes. Set aside.
3. In the same saucepan, place the zucchini noodles and cook for five minutes. Turn off the heat then add the cooked meat. Mix well.
4. Let it cool. Evenly divide into suggested servings and place in meal prep containers.

Nutrition Information:

Calories per serving: 344; Protein: 18.8g; Fat: 29.2g; Carbohydrates: 2.2g; Fiber: 0.7g

BACON-WRAPPED ROASTED ASPARAGUS

Servings per Recipe: 4
Cooking Time: 10 minutes

Ingredients:

- 16 asparagus spear, ends trimmed
- 16 pieces bacon
- 2 tablespoons extra-virgin olive oil
- Salt and pepper to taste

Directions:

1. Preheat the oven to 400⁰F.
2. Line a baking sheet with aluminum foil or parchment paper. Place the dry asparagus and place it on the baking sheet. Drizzle with olive oil and toss to coat. Add salt and pepper to taste.
3. Wrap each spear with the bacon. Bake for 10 more minutes.
4. Let it cool. Evenly divide into suggested servings and place in meal prep containers.

Nutrition Information:

Calories per serving: 139; Protein: 3.8g; Fat: 12.8g; Carbohydrates: 4.8g; Fiber: 2.0g

Simple Cod Piccata

Servings per Recipe: 3
Cooking Time: 15 minutes

Ingredients:

- 1-pound cod fillets, patted dry
- ¼ cup capers, drained
- ½ teaspoon salt
- ¾ cup chicken stock
- 1/3 cup almond flour
- 2 tablespoon fresh parsley, chopped
- 2 tablespoon grapeseed oil
- 3 tablespoon extra-virgin oil
- 3 tablespoon lemon juice

Directions:

1. In a bowl, combine together the almond flour and salt.
2. Dredge the fish in the almond flour to coat. Set aside.
3. Heat a little bit of olive oil to coat a large skillet. Heat the skillet over medium high heat. Add grapeseed oil. Cook the cod for 3 minutes on each side to brown. Remove from the plate and place on a paper towel-lined plate.
4. In a saucepan, mix together the chicken stock, capers and lemon juice. Simmer to reduce the sauce to half. Add the remaining grapeseed oil.
5. Drizzle the fried cod with the sauce and sprinkle with parsley.
6. Let it cool. Evenly divide into suggested servings and place in meal prep containers.

Nutrition Information:

Calories per serving: 269; Protein: 1.9g; Fat: 28.3g; Carbohydrates: 3.7g; Fiber: 1.5g

BAKED SALMON WITH LEMON AND THYME

Servings per Recipe: 2
Cooking Time: 15 minutes

Ingredients:

- 1-lb salmon fillet
- 1 lemon, sliced thinly
- 1 tablespoon capers, chopped
- 1 tablespoon fresh thyme, chopped
- Olive oil for drizzling
- Salt and pepper to taste

Directions:

1. Preheat the oven to 400^0F.
2. Line a baking sheet with parchment paper and place the salmon with skin side down.
3. Season the salmon with salt and pepper. Arrange the capers on top of the salmon and top with thyme and lemon slices.
4. Bake for 25 minutes.
5. Let it cool. Evenly divide into suggested servings and place in meal prep containers.

Nutrition Information:

Calories per serving: 398; Protein: 49.0g; Fat: 19.6g; Carbohydrates: 4.3g; Fiber: 0.7g

Garlic Roasted Shrimp with Zucchini Pasta

Servings per Recipe: 2

Cooking Time: 15 minutes

Ingredients:

- 8 ounces shrimp, cleaned and deveined
- 1 lemon, zested and juiced
- 2 garlic cloves, minced
- 2 medium-sized zucchini, cut into thin strips or spaghetti noodles
- 2 tablespoon ghee, melted
- 2 tablespoon olive oil
- Salt and pepper to taste

Directions:

1. Preheat the oven to 400^0F.
2. In a mixing bowl, mix all ingredients except the zucchini noodles. Toss to coat the shrimp.
3. Bake for 10 minutes until the shrimp turn pink.
4. Add the zucchini pasta then toss. Turn oven off and just leave in oven for 5 minutes.
5. Remove from oven.
6. Let it cool. Evenly divide into suggested servings and place in meal prep containers.

Nutrition Information:

Calories per serving: 357; Protein: 23.8g; Fat: 27.8g; Carbohydrates: 5.1g; Fiber: 0.6g

Keto Meal Prep Dinner Recipes

Slow Cooked Beef Pot Roast

Servings per Recipe: 4

Cooking Time: 7 hours & 20 minutes

Ingredients:

- 2 pounds beef pot roast, cut
- 2 tablespoon beef tallow
- ½ teaspoon black pepper
- ½ teaspoon dried oregano
- 1 tablespoon dried thyme
- 1 teaspoon salt
- 1 whole bay leaf
- 1 medium onion, sliced
- 3 cups water

Directions:

1. In a bowl, mix together thyme, black pepper, oregano and salt.
2. Rub the mixture all over the pot roast cut.
3. Heat a skillet and melt the beef tallow. Place the marinated pot roast and sear all sides.
4. Meanwhile, put remaining ingredients in slow cooker.
5. Add the seared pot roast and cook for 7 hours.
6. Let it cool. Evenly divide into suggested servings and place in meal prep containers.

Nutrition Information:

Calories per serving: 434; Protein: 54.9g; Fat: 23.5g; Carbohydrates: 1.6g; Fiber: 0.4g

Stuffed Instant Pot Chicken Breasts

Servings per Recipe: 2
Cooking Time: 45 minutes

Ingredients:

- 1-piece ham, halved
- 16 strips bacon
- 2 cups water
- 2 strips of skinless chicken breasts
- 4 slices mozzarella cheese
- 6 asparagus spears, trimmed
- 1 tablespoon salt

Directions:

1. Butterfly the chicken breasts by placing them on a chopping board and slicing the breasts horizontally. Place a plastic wrap over the chicken breasts and use a meat mallet to pound the breasts flatter.
2. In a mixing bowl, mix 1 tablespoon of salt and water. Soak the butterflied chicken breasts in the brine for 30 minutes. Pat dry the chicken breasts after marinating in the brine.
3. Lay the chicken breasts on a flat surface and place 1 halved of ham, 2 slices of mozzarella cheese, and 3 spears of asparagus on the center.
4. Roll up the chicken breasts and secure the edges with toothpick. Roll the bacon around the rolled chicken breasts and secure with more toothpicks.
5. Place a steamer rack or trivet in the Instant Pot and pour 1 cup of cold water. Place the chicken roll ups on the steamer rack.
6. Close the lid and select manual. Cook on high pressure for 7 minutes and do natural release. Take the roll ups out from the Instant Pot. Place the chicken roll ups in the fridge for an hour. Remove the toothpicks.
7. Drain out the pot from the water and remove the steamer rack.

8. Set the sauté setting on the Instant Pot and add the chicken roll ups. Sauté until the bacon renders its own oil.
9. Let it cool. Evenly divide into suggested servings and place in meal prep containers.

Nutrition Information:

Calories per serving: 536; Protein: 60.5g; Fat: 26.8g; Carbohydrates: 2.0g; Fiber: 0.2g

Slow Cooker Balsamic Roast Beef

Servings per Recipe: 4

Cooking Time: 8 hours

Ingredients:

- 1 ¾ pound boneless round roast
- 1 cup beef broth
- 1 tablespoon Stevia
- 1 tablespoon soy sauce
- 1 tablespoon Worcestershire sauce
- 4 cloves chopped garlic
- ¼ teaspoon red pepper flakes

Directions:

1. Place the roast beef in the slow cooker.
2. In a mixing bowl, mix all other ingredients and pour over the roast.
3. Let it sit in the slow cooker for six to eight hours.
4. Once cooked, remove from the slow cooker and break the meat apart.
5. Let it cool. Evenly divide into suggested servings and place in meal prep containers.

Nutrition Information:

Calories per serving: 354.8; Protein: 59.6g; Fat: 9.7g; Carbohydrates: 4.0g; Fiber: 0.1g

Buffalo Turkey Balls

Servings per Recipe: 5
Cooking Time: 40 minutes

Ingredients:

- 2 eggs
- 1-lb ground turkey
- ½ cup hot sauce
- ½ stick unsalted butter
- ¼ cup almond flour
- 3 tablespoon blue cheese, crumbled
- 2-oz whipped cream cheese

Directions:

1. Preheat the oven at 350 degrees Fahrenheit.
2. Mix the turkey meat, cream cheese, egg, blue cheese and almond flour in a mixing bowl. Mix well and evenly divide into 20 small meat balls.
3. Place the meat balls on a greased baking spray.
4. Bake for 15 minutes.
5. While the meatball is baking, make the sauce by mixing the butter and hot sauce in a sauce pan.
6. Remove the turkey balls from the oven and dip them in the hot sauce.
7. Place the turkey balls in the oven and re-bake for another 15 minutes.
8. Let it cool. Evenly divide into suggested servings and place in meal prep containers.

Nutrition Information:

Calories per serving: 300; Protein: 30.6g; Fat: 18.3g; Carbohydrates: 1.7g; Fiber: 0g

Stuffed Enchilada Peppers

Servings per Recipe: 6
Cooking Time: 25 minutes

Ingredients:

- 6 red or yellow peppers
- ½ cup green chilies
- 1 can fat-free plain Greek yogurt
- 1 cup fresh spinach, chopped
- 1 cup cauliflower rice
- 1-lb shredded cooked turkey or chicken breast
- 1 package shredded cheese

Directions:

1. Lightly grease a cookie sheet with cooking spray and preheat oven to 375°F.
2. Cut the tops of each pepper and remove the seeds. Set aside.
3. In a mixing bowl, mix together spinach, cheese, meat, cauliflower rice, and yogurt.
4. Fill the hollowed peppers with 2/3 of the meat mixture. Put the tops of the pepper back on.
5. Place the peppers on prepared cookie sheet and pop in the oven. Bake for 25 minutes.
6. Let it cool. Evenly divide into suggested servings and place in meal prep containers.

Nutrition Information:

Calories per serving: 305; Protein: 35.7g; Fat: 11.9g; Carbohydrates: 14.6g; Fiber: 11.9g

Keto Chicken Adobo

Servings per Recipe: 4
Cooking Time: 30 minutes

Ingredients:

- 8 skinless chicken drumsticks
- ¼ cup coconut aminos
- ½ teaspoon cracked black pepper
- 1 tablespoon olive oil
- 1 red onion, chopped
- ¼ cup vinegar
- 2 bay leaves
- ½ cup water
- 8 garlic cloves, crushed

Directions:

1. Place a medium pot on medium high heat and heat oil.
2. Once hot, sauté garlic for a minute.
3. Add onion and sauté until wilted, around 5 minutes.
4. Stir in bay leaves and cracked pepper.
5. Add chicken and sauté for 8 minutes.
6. Add coconut aminos and vinegar. Continue cooking until liquid is halved.
7. Add water, bring to a simmer, cover, and cook for 15 minutes.
8. Let it cool. Evenly divide into suggested servings and place in meal prep containers.

Nutrition Information:

Calories per serving: 476; Protein: 47.8g; Fat: 27.4g; Carbohydrates: 5.9g; Fiber: 0.9g

Balsamic Cranberry Chicken Thighs

Servings per Recipe: 4
Cooking Time: 45 minutes

Ingredients:

- 2-pounds chicken thighs, boneless and skinless
- 1 cup water
- ½ tablespoon garlic powder
- ½ tablespoon rosemary
- 1 cup cranberry, raw
- 1 red onion, chopped
- 1 tablespoon almond flour
- 1 tablespoon coconut aminos
- 1 tablespoon Worcestershire sauce
- 3 tablespoon balsamic vinegar
- Salt and pepper
- 1 tbsp oil

Directions:

1. Place a medium pot on medium high heat and heat oil.
2. While the oil is heating, season the thighs with salt and pepper. Place the chicken and brown each side for at least 5 minutes on each side. Remove and set aside.
3. Sauté the onions until it starts to caramelize. Add ¼ cup of water and scrape the browned bits on the side and bottom.
4. Place the chicken back on top of the onions and pour the cranberry sauce, balsamic vinegar, soy sauce, Worcestershire sauce, garlic powder and rosemary.
5. Place the lid, bring to a simmer, then lower heat to medium low, cover and cook for 30 minutes.
6. While the chicken is cooking, mix the cornstarch with 2 tablespoons of water.
7. Pour the slurry, mix well until it thickens.

8. Let it cool. Evenly divide into suggested servings and place in meal prep containers.

Nutrition Information:

Calories per serving: 556; Protein: 38.6g; Fat: 38.5g; Carbohydrates: 11.6g; Fiber: 2.2g

Keto Cream Cheese Chicken

Servings per Recipe: 4
Cooking Time: 15 minutes

Ingredients:

- 1 ½ pounds chicken breast, quartered
- 2/3 cup prepared Italian dressing
- 5 ½ ounces fat-free cream cheese
- 7 1/8-ounces cream of chicken soup, fat-free

Directions:

1. Place all ingredients in the Instant Pot.
2. Put the cover into place and seal.
3. Set the setting on "poultry" and set the timer for 15 minutes.
4. After 15 minutes, release the pressure for 5 minutes. Wait until all the remaining pressure has escaped from the sealed steam nozzle.
5. Let it cool. Evenly divide into suggested servings and place in meal prep containers.

Nutrition Information:

Calories per serving: 417; Protein: 56.3g; Fat: 15.4g; Carbohydrates: 9.7g; Fiber: 0.1g

Mexican Pork Carnitas

Servings per Recipe: 6

Cooking Time: 50 minutes

Ingredients:

- 2 ½ pounds pork shoulder blade roast, trimmed and bones removed
- ¼ teaspoon adobo seasoning
- ¼ teaspoon dry oregano
- ½ teaspoon garlic powder
- ¾ cup chicken broth
- 1 ½ teaspoon cumin
- 2 bay leaves
- 3 chipotle peppers
- 6 cloves garlic, slivered
- Salt and pepper to taste

Directions:

1. Season the pork with salt and pepper.
2. Heat the Instant Pot and set it to the sauté menu. Place the pork inside the pot and sear each side until brown.
3. Add the garlic, cumin, oregano, adobo sauce and garlic powder.
4. Mix well then pour the chicken broth and chipotle peppers.
5. Add the bay leaves and continue stirring.
6. Cover with the lid and cook on high for 30 minutes.
7. Once the timer sets off, do quick release and shred the pork using two forks.
8. Place the pork back and let it simmer for another 10 minutes.
9. Let it cool. Evenly divide into suggested servings and place in meal prep containers.

Nutrition Information:

Calories per serving: 431.5; Protein: 49.6g; Fat: 22.7g; Carbohydrates: 4.6g; Fiber: 0.6g

Garlic Pork Chops

Servings per Recipe: 4

Cooking Time: 25 minutes

Ingredients:

- 4 ¾ inch boneless pork chops
- 1 ½ cups chicken broth
- 1 tablespoon butter
- 1 tablespoon olive oil
- 2 lemons, juiced
- 6 cloves garlic, minced
- Garlic powder
- Salt and pepper to taste

Directions:

1. Set the Instant Pot to sauté and heat the olive oil.
2. Season the pork with salt, pepper and garlic powder.
3. Place the pork in the Instant Pot and brown the sides. Set aside.
4. Add the garlic and sauté for a minute. Add the lemon juice and chicken broth. Stir in the butter.
5. Add the pork chops back to the pan. Cover the lid and set it to manual. Cook on high for 10 minutes.
6. Let it rest before doing a quick release.
7. Let it cool. Evenly divide into suggested servings and place in meal prep containers.

Nutrition Information:

Calories per serving: 355; Protein: 50.2g; Fat: 14.0g; Carbohydrates: 4.8g; Fiber: 0.3g

Apple Bacon BBQ Pulled Pork

Servings per Recipe: 6
Cooking Time: 35 minutes

Ingredients:

- 2-pounds lean pork tenderloin, fat removed
- 2 tomatoes chopped
- 1 ½ cup onion, chopped
- 1 medium apple, peeled and chopped
- 1/3 cup Worcestershire sauce
- 2 teaspoons salt
- 3 tablespoon apple cider vinegar
- 4 packets Stevia
- 4 slices bacon, chopped

Directions:

1. Set the Instant Pot to sauté. Add the chopped bacon and render until the fat is released and bacon is crisp. Remove the bacon pieces and place them on a plate lined with paper towel.
2. Sauté the onions, tomatoes, and apples. Add the Stevia, Worcestershire sauce, salt and cider vinegar. Add the bacon and pork.
3. Cover with the lid and set the Instant Pot on high for 25 minutes.
4. Release the pressure to open the lid and shred the pork using two forks. Return the pork to the sauce to coat.
5. Let it cool. Evenly divide into suggested servings and place in meal prep containers.

Nutrition Information:

Calories per serving: 335; Protein: 42.5g; Fat: 12.3g; Carbohydrates: 12.3g; Fiber: 1.7g

Beefy Cabbage Bowls

Servings per Recipe: 4
Cooking Time: 20 minutes

Ingredients:

- 1-pound lean ground beef
- ½ teaspoon paprika
- 1 cup beef broth
- 1 cup cauliflower rice
- 1 garlic clove, minced
- 1 medium head cabbage, cored and chopped
- 1 tablespoon dried marjoram
- 2 tablespoon raisins
- 8-ounces tomato sauce
- Cooking spray
- Salt and pepper to taste

Directions:

1. Choose the sauté button on the Instant Pot and spray with oil and add the beef. Season with salt and pepper. Cook the beef until it is browned. Add the garlic and marjoram. Cook for a few minutes.
2. Add the tomato sauce, beef broth, paprika and raisins.
3. Close the lid and cook on high pressure for 15 minutes.
4. Press the quick release and add the rice and cabbage and cook on 3 minutes for high pressure.
5. Let it cool. Evenly divide into suggested servings and place in meal prep containers.

Nutrition Information:

Calories per serving: 313; Protein: 33.9g; Fat: 13.2g; Carbohydrates: 15.8g; Fiber: 4.4g

Lamb Curry Stew with Artichoke Hearts

Servings per Recipe: 4
Cooking Time: 30 minutes

Ingredients:

- 2-pounds lamb leg, trimmed from fat and cut into chunks
- ½ teaspoon black pepper
- ½ teaspoon curry powder
- ½ teaspoon ground cinnamon
- 1 clove garlic, minced
- 1 cup canned beef broth
- 2 tablespoons onion powder
- 1 tablespoon curry powder
- 1 tablespoon fresh lemon juice
- 1 tablespoon olive oil
- 1 teaspoon garam masala
- 1 teaspoon salt
- 1/3 cup manzanilla olives
- 14 ½ ounce heat roasted diced tomatoes
- 14-ounces artichoke hearts, quartered
- 2 teaspoon ginger root, grated

Directions:

1. In a bowl, combine the lamb meat with salt, pepper and ½ tablespoon of curry.
2. Set the Instant Pot to sauté setting and heat the olive oil. Place the lamb meat and sauté until all sides are brown. Remove from the pot and set aside.
3. Sauté garlic and ginger for a minute or two. Pour the broth and scrape the sides or bottoms from the browning. Add the lamb back and place the rest of the ingredients except for the lemon juice.
4. Cover the lid and set to manual. Cook on high for 12 minutes.

5. Use the quick pressure release to open the lid.
6. Add in the lemon juice and let it boil for another 5 minutes.
7. Let it cool. Evenly divide into suggested servings and place in meal prep containers.

Nutrition Information:

Calories per serving: 434; Protein: 51.2g; Fat: 17.3g; Carbohydrates: 19.5g; Fiber: 8.2g

Stir Fried Asian Beef

Servings per Recipe: 4

Cooking Time: 25 minutes

Ingredients:

- 2-pounds flank steak, cut into strips
- ½ cup coconut aminos
- ½ cup water
- ½ teaspoon minced ginger
- 1 tablespoon vegetable oil
- 2 tablespoons almond flour + 3 tablespoons water
- 5 packets Stevia or more to taste
- 3 green onions, sliced
- 4 cloves garlic, minced

Directions:

1. Place a wok or large nonstick fry pan on high heat and let it heat. Once hot add oil and wait for two minutes.
2. Meanwhile, in a bowl season beef strips with pepper and salt.
3. Add seasoned beef to pan and stir fry for 5 minutes or until browned. Transfer to a plate.
4. Lower heat to medium high and sauté garlic for a minute.
5. Stir in ginger, Stevia, coconut aminos, and water. Mix well.
6. Return beef, cover and cook around 12 minutes.
7. Meanwhile, combine almond flour and water. Mix into pan and stir well. Cook until sauce has thickened.
8. Garnish with green onions.
9. Let it cool. Evenly divide into suggested servings and place in meal prep containers.

Nutrition Information:

Calories per serving: 354; Protein: 49.1g; Fat: 14.9g; Carbohydrates: 2.7g; Fiber: 0.6g

Keto Meal Prep Dessert/Snack Recipes

Cardamom and Cinnamon Fat Bombs

Servings per Recipe: 10
Cooking Time: 3 minutes

Ingredients:

- ¼ tsp ground cardamom (green)
- ¼ tsp ground cinnamon
- ½ cup unsweetened shredded coconut
- ½ tsp vanilla extract
- 3-oz unsalted butter, room temperature

Directions:

1. Place a nonstick pan on medium heat and toast coconut until lightly browned.
2. In a bowl, mix all ingredients.
3. Evenly roll into 10 equal balls.
4. Let it cool in the fridge.
5. Store in an airtight meal prep container.

Nutrition Information:

Calories per serving: 90; Protein: 0.4g; Fat: 10g; Carbohydrates: 0.4g; Fiber: 1.0g

Keto-Approved Cheese Chips

Servings per Recipe: 4
Cooking Time: 8 minutes

Ingredients:

- 8 oz. cheddar, provolone, or edam cheese, in slices
- ½ tsp paprika powder

Directions:

1. Line baking sheet with foil and preheat oven to 400°F.
2. Place cheese slices on baking sheet and sprinkle paprika powder on top.
3. Pop in the oven and bake for 8 to 10 minutes.
4. Pay particular attention when timer reaches 6 to 7 minutes as a burnt cheese tastes bitter.
5. Let it cool. Evenly divide into suggested servings and place in meal prep containers.

Nutrition Information:

Calories per serving: 228; Protein: 13.0g; Fat: 19.0g; Carbohydrates: 2.0g; Fiber: 0g

Cheese Roll-Ups the Keto Way

Servings per Recipe: 4
Cooking Time: 0 minutes

Ingredients:

- 4 slices cheddar cheese
- 4 ham slices

Directions:

1. Place one cheese slice on a flat surface and top with one slice of ham.
2. Roll from one end to the other. Repeat process to remaining cheese and ham.
3. Evenly divide into suggested servings and place in meal prep containers.

Nutrition Information:

Calories per serving: 60; Protein: 6.7g; Fat: 2.6g; Carbohydrates: 2.5g; Fiber: 0g

Bacon and Cheddar Cheese Balls

Servings per Recipe: 10

Cooking Time: 8 minutes

Ingredients:

- 5 1⁄3-oz bacon
- 5 1⁄3-oz cheddar cheese
- 5 1⁄3-oz cream cheese
- ½ tsp chili flakes (optional)
- ½ tsp pepper (optional)

Directions:

1. Pan fry bacon until crisped, around 8 minutes.
2. Meanwhile, in a food processor, process remaining ingredients. Then transfer to a bowl and refrigerate. When ready to handle, form into 20 equal balls.
3. Once bacon is cooked, crumble bacon and spread on a plate.
4. Roll the balls on the crumbled bacon to coat.
5. Store in airtight meal prep containers.

Nutrition Information:

Calories per serving: 225.6; Protein: 6.4g; Fat: 21.6g; Carbohydrates: 1.6g; Fiber: 0g

Flaxseed, Maple & Pumpkin Muffin

Servings per Recipe: 10
Cooking Time: 20 minutes

Ingredients:

- 1 tbsp cinnamon
- 1 cup pure pumpkin puree
- 1 tbsp pumpkin pie spice
- 2 tbsp coconut oil
- 1 egg
- 1/2 tbsp baking powder
- 1/2 tsp salt
- 1/2 tsp apple cider vinegar
- 1/2 tsp vanilla extract
- 1/3 cup erythritol
- 1 1/4 cup flaxseeds (ground)
- 1/4 cup Walden Farm's Maple Syrup

Directions:

1. Line ten muffin tins with ten muffin liners and preheat oven to 350°F.
2. In a blender, add all ingredients and blend until smooth and creamy, around 5 minutes.
3. Evenly divide batter into prepared muffin tins.
4. Pop in the oven and bake for 20 minutes or until tops are lightly browned.
5. Let it cool. Evenly divide into suggested servings and place in meal prep containers.

Nutrition Information:

Calories per serving: 120; Protein: 5.0g; Fat: 8.5g; Carbohydrates: 5.0g; Fiber: 3.0g

Spiced Devilled Eggs

Servings per Recipe: 6

Cooking Time: 8 minutes

Ingredients:

- 6 eggs
- ¼ tsp salt
- ½ cup mayonnaise
- ½ tbsp poppy seeds
- 1 tbsp red curry paste

Directions:

1. Place eggs in a small pot and add enough water to cover it. Bring to a boil without a cover, lower heat to a simmer and simmer for 8 minutes.
2. Immediately dunk in ice cold water once done cooking. Peel egg shells and slice eggs in half lengthwise.
3. Remove yolks and place them in a medium bowl. Add the rest of the ingredients in the bowl except for the egg whites. Mix well.
4. Evenly return the yolk mixture into the middle of the egg whites.
5. Let it cool. Evenly divide into suggested servings and place in meal prep containers.

Nutrition Information:

Calories per serving: 200; Protein: 6.0g; Fat: 19.0g; Carbohydrates: 1.0g; Fiber: 0g

Keto Reese Cups

Servings per Recipe: 12

Cooking Time: 1 minute

Ingredients:

- ½ cup unsweetened shredded coconut
- 1 cup almond butter
- 1 cup dark chocolate chips
- 1 tablespoon coconut oil
- 1 tablespoon Stevia

Directions:

1. Line 12 muffin tins with 12 muffin liners.
2. Place the almond butter, honey and oil in a glass bowl and microwave for 30 seconds or until melted. Divide the mixture into 12 muffin tins. Let it cool for 30 minutes in the fridge.
3. Add the shredded coconuts and mix until evenly distributed.
4. Pour the remaining melted chocolate on top of the coconuts. Freeze for an hour.
5. Carefully remove the chocolates from the muffin tins to create perfect Reese cups.
6. Store in airtight meal prep containers.

Nutrition Information:

Calories per serving: 214; Protein: 5.0g; Fat: 17.1g; Carbohydrates: 13.7g; Fiber: 3.1g

No Cook Coconut and Chocolate Bars

Servings per Recipe: 6

Cooking Time: 0 minutes

Ingredients:

- 1 tbsp Stevia
- ¾ cup shredded coconut, unsweetened
- ½ cup ground nuts (almonds, pecans, or walnuts)
- ¼ cup unsweetened cocoa powder
- 4 tbsps coconut oil

Directions:

1. In a medium bowl, mix shredded coconut, nuts and cocoa powder.
2. Add Stevia and coconut oil.
3. Mix batter thoroughly.
4. In a 9x9 square inch pan or dish, press the batter and for 30-minutes place in the freezer.
5. Evenly divide into suggested servings and place in meal prep containers.

Nutrition Information:

Calories per serving: 148; Protein: 1.6g; Fat: 7.8g; Carbohydrates: 2.3g; Fiber: 1.1g

Keto-Approved Trail Mix

Servings per Recipe: 8

Cooking Time: 3 minutes

Ingredients:

- ½ cup salted pumpkin seeds
- ½ cup slivered almonds
- ¾ cup roasted pecan halves
- ¾ cup unsweetened cranberries
- 1 cup toasted coconut flakes

Directions:

1. In a skillet, place almonds and pecans. Heat for 2-3 minutes and let cool.
2. Once cooled, in a large re-sealable plastic bag, combine all ingredients.
3. Seal and shake vigorously to mix.
4. Evenly divide into suggested servings and store in airtight meal prep containers.

Nutrition Information:

Calories per serving: 184; Protein: 4.4g; Fat: 14.4g; Carbohydrates: 13.0g; Fiber: 2.8g

Onion Cheese Muffins

Servings per Recipe: 6
Cooking Time: 20 minutes

Ingredients:

- ¼ cup Colby jack cheese, shredded
- ¼ cup shallots, minced
- ½ tsp salt
- 1 cup almond flour
- 1 egg
- 3 tbsp melted butter
- 3 tbsp sour cream

Directions:

1. Line 6 muffin tins with 6 muffin liners. Set aside and preheat oven to 350°F.
2. In a bowl, stir the dry and wet ingredients alternately. Mix well using a spatula until the consistency of the mixture becomes even.
3. Scoop a spoonful of the batter to the prepared muffin tins.
4. Bake for 20 minutes in oven until golden brown.
5. Let it cool and store in an airtight container.

Nutrition Information:

Calories per serving: 193; Protein: 6.3g; Fat: 17.4g; Carbohydrates: 4.6g; Fiber: 2.1g

Bacon-Flavored Kale Chips

Servings per Recipe: 6
Cooking Time: 25 minutes

Ingredients:

- 1-lb kale, around 1 bunch
- 1 to 2 tsp salt
- 2 tbsp butter
- ¼ cup bacon grease

Directions:

1. Remove the rib from kale leaves and tear into 2-inch pieces.
2. Clean the kale leaves thoroughly and dry them inside a salad spinner.
3. In a skillet, add the butter to the bacon grease and warm the two fats under low heat. Add salt and stir constantly.
4. Set aside and let it cool.
5. Put the dried kale in a Ziploc back and add the cool liquid bacon grease and butter mixture.
6. Seal the Ziploc back and gently shake the kale leaves with the butter mixture. The leaves should have this shiny consistency which means that they are coated evenly with the fat.
7. Pour the kale leaves on a cookie sheet and sprinkle more salt if necessary.
8. Bake for 25 minutes inside a preheated 350-degree oven or until the leaves start to turn brown as well as crispy.
9. Let it cool, evenly divide into suggested servings and store in an airtight container.

Nutrition Information:

Calories per serving: 148; Protein: 3.3g; Fat: 13.1g; Carbohydrates: 6.6g; Fiber: 2.7g

WALNUT & PUMPKIN SPICE KETO BREAD

Servings per Recipe: 12 slices
Cooking Time: 60 minutes

Ingredients:

- 4 large eggs
- 2 cups almond flour
- 1 tbsp baking powder
- 1 pinch sea salt
- 1 cup pumpkin puree
- 1/2 cup coconut flour (sifted)
- 1/2 cup erythritol
- 1/3 cup heavy cream
- 1/4 cup chopped walnuts
- 3/4 cup melted butter
- 1 1/2 tsp pumpkin pie spice

Directions:

1. Lightly grease a loaf pan and preheat oven to 350°F.
2. In a large mixing bowl, whisk well salt, pumpkin spice, baking powder, sugar free sweetener, coconut flour, and almond flour.
3. In a blender, blend until smooth the eggs, heavy cream, butter, and pumpkin.
4. Pour into bowl of dry ingredients and mix thoroughly.
5. Pour batter in loaf pan and bake for 60 minutes or when poked with a toothpick, it comes out clean.
6. Remove bread from pan.
7. Let it cool. Evenly divide into suggested servings and place in meal prep containers.

Nutrition Information:

Calories per serving: 230; Protein: 5.5g; Fat: 20g; Carbohydrates: 6.5g; Fiber: 2.0g

Low Carb Keto Peanut Butter Cookies

Servings per Recipe: 24
Cooking Time: 15 minutes

Ingredients:

- 2 large eggs
- ¼ tsp salt
- 1 cup unsweetened peanut butter
- 1 tsp baking soda
- 1 tsp stevia powder
- 1/8 tsp xanthan gum
- 2 cups almond flour
- 2 tbsp butter
- 2 tsp pure vanilla extract
- 4 ounces softened cream cheese
- 5 drops liquid Splenda

Directions:

1. Line a cookie sheet with a non-stick liner. Set aside.
2. In a bowl, mix xanthan gum, flour, salt and baking soda. Set aside.
3. On a mixing bowl, combine the butter, cream cheese and peanut butter.
4. Mix on high speed until it forms a smooth consistency. Add the sweetener. Add the eggs and vanilla gradually while mixing until it forms a smooth consistency.
5. Add the almond flour mixture slowly and mix until well combined.
6. The dough is ready once it starts to stick together into a ball.
7. Scoop the dough using a 1 tablespoon cookie scoop and drop each cookie on the prepared cookie sheet. You will make around 24 cookies
8. Press the cookie with a fork and bake for 10 to 12 minutes at 350°F.
9. Let it cool and place in an airtight container.

Nutrition Information:

Calories per serving: 91.2; Protein: 3.7g; Fat: 6.8g; Carbohydrates: 4.7g; Fiber: 0.7g

CAULIFLOWER, CHEDDAR & JALAPENO MUFFINS

Servings per Recipe: 12

Cooking Time: 30 minutes

Ingredients:

- 1 cup grated cheddar cheese
- 1 cup grated mozzarella cheese
- 1 Tbsp dried onion flakes
- 1/2 tsp baking powder
- 1/2 tsp garlic powder
- 1/3 cup grated parmesan cheese
- 1/4 cup coconut flour
- 1/4 tsp black pepper
- 1/4 tsp salt
- 2 cups finely riced, raw cauliflower
- 2 eggs, beaten
- 2 Tbsp melted butter
- 2 Tbsp minced jalapeno

Directions:

1. Line 12 muffin tins with muffin cups and preheat oven to 375oF.
2. In a medium bowl, whisk well eggs. Stir in coconut flour, baking powder, garlic powder, pepper, salt, onion flakes, cheese, melted butter, jalapeno, and cauliflower. Mix thoroughly.
3. Evenly divide into prepared muffin tins.
4. Pop in the oven and bake for 30 minutes.
5. Let it cool. Evenly divide into suggested servings and place in meal prep containers.

Nutrition Information:

Calories per serving: 110; Protein: 8g; Fat: 8g; Carbohydrates: 3.8g; Fiber: 2g

Keto Choco-Chia Pudding

Servings per Recipe: 2
Cooking Time: 0 minutes

Ingredients:

- 1 tsp Stevia (optional)
- ¼ cup fresh or frozen raspberries
- 1 scoop chocolate protein powder
- 1 cup unsweetened almond milk
- 3 tbsp Chia seeds

Directions:

1. Mix the chocolate protein powder and almond milk.
2. Add the chia seeds and mix well with a whisk or a fork.
3. Flavor with Stevia depending on the desired sweetness.
4. Let it rest for 5 minutes and continue stirring.
5. Place in meal prep containers and let it cool in the fridge for at least an hour.

Nutrition Information:

Calories per serving: 143.5; Protein: 11.5g; Fat: 4.7g; Carbohydrates: 14.6g; Fiber: 4.8g

Ketogenic Diet 3 Week Meal Plan

Week 1: Shopping List

- 1 cup pure pumpkin puree
- 16 eggs
- 1-lb ground beef
- 1-lb ground turkey meat
- 1-piece ham, halved
- 2 cups spinach
- 2 kale leaves
- 2 strips of skinless chicken breasts
- 2-oz whipped cream cheese
- Blue cheese
- 30 grams blueberries
- 4 boneless pork chops
- 4 large egg whites, beaten
- 4 slices mozzarella cheese
- 5 medium-sized mushrooms
- 6 asparagus spears
- 8 skinless chicken drumsticks
- Almond flour
- Almond milk
- Apple cider vinegar
- Bacon
- Baking powder
- Bay leaves
- Black pepper
- Broccoli
- Butter
- Cayenne pepper
- Chinese five spices
- Cinnamon
- Coconut aminos
- Coconut cream or coconut milk or sour cream
- Coconut flour
- Coconut oil
- Erythritol
- Fish sauce
- Five spice powder
- Flaxseeds (ground)
- Fresh basil
- Garlic cloves
- Hot sauce
- Lemongrass
- Olive oil
- Onions
- Pepper corn
- Pumpkin pie spice
- Red bell pepper
- Salt
- Sambal chili paste
- Sesame oil
- Soy sauce
- Star anise
- Stevia
- Sugar-free ketchup

- Vanilla extract
- Vinegar
- Walden farm's maple syrup
- Water

Week 1: Meal Plan

Day One:

Breakfast - Buttered Basil on Scrambled Egg

Lunch - Hashed Brussels Sprouts

Dinner - Stuffed Instant Pot Chicken Breasts

Snacks/Desserts - Flaxseed, Maple & Pumpkin Muffin

Day Two:

Breakfast - Keto Spinach Frittata

Lunch - Asian-Inspired Keto Pork Chops

Dinner - Buffalo Turkey Balls

Snacks/Desserts

Day Three:

Breakfast - Buttered Basil on Scrambled Egg

Lunch - Stir-Fried Ground Beef

Dinner - Keto Chicken Adobo

Snacks/Desserts - Flaxseed, Maple & Pumpkin Muffin

Day Four:

Breakfast - Keto Spinach Frittata

Lunch - Hashed Brussels Sprouts

Dinner - Buffalo Turkey Balls

Snacks/Desserts - Flaxseed, Maple & Pumpkin Muffin

Day Five:

Breakfast - Keto-Approved Blueberry Pancakes

Lunch - Asian-Inspired Keto Pork Chops

Dinner - Keto Chicken Adobo
Snacks/Desserts - Flaxseed, Maple & Pumpkin Muffin

Day Six:
Breakfast - Keto Spinach Frittata
Lunch - Stir-Fried Ground Beef
Dinner - Buffalo Turkey Balls
Snacks/Desserts - Flaxseed, Maple & Pumpkin Muffin

Day Seven:
Breakfast - Keto-Approved Blueberry Pancakes
Lunch - Hashed Brussels Sprouts
Dinner - Stuffed Instant Pot Chicken Breasts
Snacks/Desserts - Flaxseed, Maple & Pumpkin Muffin

WEEK 2: SHOPPING LIST

- 1 asparagus
- 1 can fat-free plain Greek yogurt
- 17 eggs
- 1-lb shredded cooked turkey or chicken breast
- 2 filets Mahi Mahi fish
- 2 pounds beef pot roast cut
- 2 pounds beef short ribs
- 2-pounds lean pork tenderloin, fat removed
- 4 tbsp hummus
- 9 mushrooms
- Almond butter
- Apple
- Apple cider vinegar
- Bacon
- Bay leaf
- Beef tallow
- Black pepper
- Butter
- Cauliflower
- Cheddar cheese
- Coconut aminos
- Coconut oil
- Curry powder
- Dark chocolate chips
- Dried oregano
- Dried thyme
- Fresh coriander
- Fresh spinach
- Green chilies
- Ham slices
- Lime
- Milk
- Olive oil
- Onion
- Parmesan cheese
- Philadelphia cheese
- Red or yellow peppers
- Salt
- Sesame oil
- Shredded cheese
- Star anise
- Stevia
- Szechuan peppercorns
- Tomatoes
- Unsweetened shredded coconut
- Water
- Worcestershire sauce
- Yellow onion

WEEK 2: MEAL PLAN

DAY ONE:

Breakfast - Mushroom Omelet Keto Approved

Lunch - Chicken Coconut Curry

Dinner - Slow Cooked Beef Pot Roast

Snacks/Desserts - Paleo Reese Cups

DAY TWO:

Breakfast - Keto Asparagus Frittata

Lunch - Steamed Mahi-Mahi with Hummus

Dinner - Stuffed Enchilada Peppers

Snacks/Desserts - Cheese Roll-Ups the Keto Way

DAY THREE:

Breakfast - Mushroom Omelet Keto Approved

Lunch - Asian Beef Short Ribs

Dinner - Apple Bacon BBQ Pulled Pork

Snacks/Desserts - Paleo Reese Cups

DAY FOUR:

Breakfast - Keto Asparagus Frittata

Lunch - Chicken Coconut Curry

Dinner - Slow Cooked Beef Pot Roast

Snacks/Desserts - Cheese Roll-Ups the Keto Way

DAY FIVE:

Breakfast - Keto Asparagus Frittata

Lunch - Asian Beef Short Ribs

Dinner - Apple Bacon BBQ Pulled Pork

Snacks/Desserts - Paleo Reese Cups

Day Six:

Breakfast - Mushroom Omelet Keto Approved

Lunch - Steamed Mahi-Mahi with Hummus

Dinner - Stuffed Enchilada Peppers

Snacks/Desserts - Cheese Roll-Ups the Keto Way

Day Seven:

Breakfast - Keto Asparagus Frittata

Lunch - Asian Beef Short Ribs

Dinner - Slow Cooked Beef Pot Roast

Snacks/Desserts - Paleo Reese Cups

Week 3: Shopping List

- ¼-Lb ham
- 1 ½ pounds chicken breast
- 1 ½ pounds ground pork
- 1 medium head cabbage
- 1/2-pound lean ground beef
- 16 asparagus spears
- 16 pieces bacon
- 17 eggs
- 1-lb salmon fillet
- 1-pound lean ground beef
- 2 eggs
- 2 heads cauliflower
- 2-pounds flank steak, cut into strips
- 3 green onions, sliced
- 4 medium-sized zucchinis
- 5 ½ ounces fat-free cream cheese
- 8 ounces shrimp
- 8-ounces tomato sauce
- Almond flour
- Baking powder
- Beef broth
- Black pepper
- Capers
- Cheddar cheese
- Cherry tomatoes
- Chia seeds
- Chocolate protein powder
- Cilantro
- Coconut aminos
- Coconut flour
- Cooking spray
- Cream of chicken soup, fat-free
- Dried marjoram
- Dried onion flakes
- Dried oregano
- Extra-virgin olive oil
- Fresh or frozen raspberries
- Fresh thyme
- Freshly ground black pepper
- Garlic
- Garlic powder
- Ghee
- Ginger
- Grated parmesan cheese
- Heavy cream
- Italian dressing
- Jalapeno
- Keto taco seasoning
- Kosher salt
- Lemon
- Melted butter
- Mozzarella cheese
- Paprika
- Raisins
- Red pepper flakes

- Shredded cheddar
- Stevia
- Unsweetened almond milk
- Vegetable oil
- Water

Week 3: Meal Plan

Day One:

Breakfast - Keto-Approved Burrito Breakfast Bowl

Lunch - Garlic Roasted Shrimp with Zucchini Pasta

Dinner - Beefy Cabbage Bowls

Snacks/Desserts - Keto Choco-Chia Pudding

Day Two:

Breakfast - Egg Cups Wrapped in Zucchini

Lunch - Baked Salmon with Lemon and Thyme

Dinner - Keto Cream Cheese Chicken

Snacks/Desserts - Cauliflower, Cheddar & Jalapeno Muffins

Day Three:

Breakfast - Traditional Scotch Eggs Recipe

Lunch - Garlic Roasted Shrimp with Zucchini Pasta

Dinner - Stir Fried Asian Beef

Snacks/Desserts - Cauliflower, Cheddar & Jalapeno Muffins

Day Four:

Breakfast - Egg Cups Wrapped in Zucchini

Lunch - Bacon-Wrapped Roasted Asparagus

Dinner - Beefy Cabbage Bowls

Snacks/Desserts - Keto Choco-Chia Pudding

Day Five:

Breakfast - Keto-Approved Burrito Breakfast Bowl

Lunch - Baked Salmon with Lemon and Thyme

Dinner - Keto Cream Cheese Chicken

Snacks/Desserts - Cauliflower, Cheddar & Jalapeno Muffins

Day Six:

Breakfast - Egg Cups Wrapped in Zucchini

Lunch - Bacon-Wrapped Roasted Asparagus

Dinner - Beefy Cabbage Bowls

Snacks/Desserts - Cauliflower, Cheddar & Jalapeno Muffins

Day Seven:

Breakfast - Traditional Scotch Eggs Recipe

Lunch - Bacon-Wrapped Roasted Asparagus

Dinner - Stir Fried Asian Beef

Snacks/Desserts - Cauliflower, Cheddar & Jalapeno Muffins

Conclusion

Your journey does not end here. In fact, it has barely started. I hope you will enjoy whipping up these recipes in your kitchen—as much as I did! Remember, all the recipes here are easy to follow. You do not need to be a chef to duplicate them in your very own kitchen.

Enjoy the food and most of all enjoy the journey to a slimmer you!

CPSIA information can be obtained
at www.ICGtesting.com
Printed in the USA
LVHW101502310720
662088LV00017B/358